Ellen van Neerven (born in Meanjin, 1990) is an award-winning writer and editor of Mununjali Yugambeh (South East Queensland) and Dutch heritage. Ellen's first book, *Heat and Light*, was the recipient of the David Unaipon Award, the Dobbie Literary Award and the NSW Premier's Literary Awards Indigenous Writers Prize. They have written two poetry collections: *Comfort Food*, which was shortlisted for the NSW Premier's Literary Awards Kenneth Slessor Prize; and *Throat*, which won the Kenneth Slessor Prize, the Multicultural NSW Award and Book of the Year at the NSW Premier's Literary Awards, and was shortlisted for the Queensland Literary Awards, the Victorian Premier's Literary Awards and the ALS Gold Medal.

Also by Ellen van Neerven

Comfort Food
Heat and Light
Flock (editor)
Homeland Calling (editor)

THROAT

ELLEN VAN NEERVEN

UQP

First published 2020 by University of Queensland Press
PO Box 6042, St Lucia, Queensland 4067 Australia
Reprinted 2020, 2021 (twice), 2023

University of Queensland Press (UQP) acknowledges the Traditional Owners
and their custodianship of the lands on which UQP operates. We pay our respects
to their Ancestors and their descendants, who continue cultural and spiritual
connections to Country. We recognise their valuable contributions to Australian
and global society.

uqp.com.au
reception@uqp.com.au

Cover design and illustration by Josh Durham (Design by Committee)
Author photograph by Anna Jacobson
Typeset in 11.5/14 pt Adobe Garamond by Post Pre-press Group, Brisbane
Printed in Australia by McPherson's Printing Group

 The University of Queensland Press is supported by the
Queensland Government through Arts Queensland.

 The University of Queensland Press is
assisted by the Australian Government
through the Australia Council, its arts
funding and advisory body.

A catalogue record for this book is available from the National Library of Australia.

ISBN 978 0 7022 6291 3 (pbk)
ISBN 978 0 7022 6434 4 (epdf)

no-one's found
until they find themselves hurting
in the back of the throat

— Patience Agbabi

they haunt-walk in

Memories sometimes come backwards. They haunt-walk in. My therapist – in our last session together before she left – asked me to describe the creative process. I said a voice to throw belief at. How I sit at one side of the table to tip tap on the laptop and the other to write in my notebook. This morning I faced an identity crisis organising my wardrobe. It is mid-spring and I'm not yet warm. In my home, my Country – now several hundred kilometres north-east from here – the sun sits on my shoulders. Every breath is a loss or gain of water. Here, my legs curl to my knees and my throat is always dry.

Memories sometimes come backwards. They haunt-walk in. Haunting, walking, and sugar from the chocolates my friends give me after 'the incident'. 'We are in great admiration of how you handled yourself. We thought you conducted yourself with such dignity and grace.' I did nothing but lie in my bed. As I search for a card in the chocolate box, something tells me I'm not meant to hear about what people think about me – this kind of aggrieved love – until I'm dead. So I'm walking-dead-haunting-live and there seems nothing left to do but write about my trauma. My therapist has left and I haven't done my hw for my osteo. My inbox is full of sympathy and unsympathetic requests.

Memories sometimes come backwards. They haunt-walk in. Writing around trauma is easy when the commissions keep coming. I'm flirting with myself, my reflection in the glass door does not need to ask for my number. My laptop screen greens with displeased fingers. After 'the incident' my gf spends time weeding my emails, we are e-entwined. If I get a +ve one I promise to respond in 2–30 days. If I get a -ve one I promise to screenshot.

18Cs

1.
calves strung on the massage table
my body's caught in a bad memory, she says
it can be overcome
she says I respond well to firm pressure
let this be my response.

2.
Carlton: walking to my new residence
take three steps through what looks like fingers and blood
before I register: chips and sauce
trams are waiting.

3.
community was so welcoming. it felt like my welcome here.

4.
sovereignty was never ceded. why do we need to reference
the invasion, we are continuing our ancestors' talk. I
can close my eyes and you are gone – that's the power of
Country.

5.
cut my hair today with nurses' scissors for it's my health I
consider. where did the words on the street come from? and
what will take away their protection? it's just hair.

6.

commission into black deaths in custody, commission to
write my name out a bunch of ways, to write a blog on
safety, commission into black deaths in custody, my skull
size was commissioned, my heartlines were commissioned.
this was a commission too.

7.

copycats are back. what you told my grandmother you told
my mother you told me. there's a crossover of words and
tones and spins. copycats are back.

8.

careful with the way I pick up a pen, careful with my words,
Mum taught me that, culture taught me that.

9.

culture can not be multi not even for a politician's
convenience not even for a white man's lie. still selling but
the world's cottoning on.

10.

class was nice, instructor was poetic, said practice was like
coming home. noticed girl with sky blue jumper. saw her in
the organics store after. mentioned jumper's colour. she said
it was like the walls of her first bedroom. a double comfort,
I said, and helped her find ingredients for an orange almond
cake until she said it was for her boyfriend.

11.

created communities are a way to design our futures.

12.

colourblind is a common complaint. you claim you don't see
colour. how about I show you the colours on the awnings of
your church, the posts of your university, the gates on your
homes. let me illuminate this cos you're in the dark.

13.

chills. they didn't bury you right.

14.

cost-effective Friday night dinners – how about I drink the
salted water I soaked my toes in, how about I call Blackfella
Eats and ask them where the yams are, how about?

15.

Citizen was waiting for me at the bookstore. becoming a
habit to walk home with brown paper parcels. I'm looking
for comfort now my protection has gone. I've grown up
to a world that was uglier than the one I was promised.
I remember days where I would skip home. my feet would
get this much off the ground. tell me where did all that
hope go?

16.

can we be post-gravity too? post-cop-killers and
post-take-the-children-away?

17.

coast trip tomorrow can't wait to be on the waves and see
my location with a bit more perspective.

18.
courage is telling them what you think of that play. that
script they try and write us in will no longer contain us.
bring me a new coat of oppression. this one's wearing thin.

logonliveon

She's warned about that app. *Watch out, you'll get addicted.* As the Aboriginal flag begins to populate the screen, she doesn't know where to look.

who is the danger

who is in real danger

the ones who say nothing

scared of dying online

show me what is in front of your eyes
rain on the deck
skating through to the other side

what sits in front of your eyes
will make its way behind your mind
they will make a movement out of you

if facebook is poetry
who will step out of the dying web

the new nuclear
log on / enter the black hole
what are you willing to put out there to save yourself

I don't want to be a *statusnative*

flesh-eating
deafening
delete to live
defeat the white noise

here is a safe space online
log on / find out what you don't know
if you knew what people were thinking of you
you'd shrink yourself
into an avatar

for all the blank screens
tiddas brothers
'not known'

there was a time when I was and now I'm not
my screen has gone blank

for all that's been gone through
tiddas brothers
'not known'

we don't get to choose our grief
if you want to pick at mine
try it on

in a socially fragile future
what will you say about you
what will you say about me
what will we remember?

Chermy

Westfield Chermy is one of our sacred sites / ehh gammin! /
my grandparents came to Chermy in the early 50s / they
had a house on Fee St / where my mother and her siblings
grew up / they moved there after the two older children
were born in Wacol / Mum was the second born in Fee St.

The shopping centre first opened in 1957 / Chermside
Drive-in Shopping Centre / now it's the largest single-level
shopping centre in Australia / it expanded / and expanded /
expanded / over years.

Mum remembers / an oval surrounded by bush / swimming
pool in the middle.

On the weekends she and her brothers and sisters had the
choice / go to the pool / or the cinema / The Dawn opened in
1928 / shut in 2005 / the last single-screen cinema in Brisbane.

Round Chermy everything's changed / some parts
unrecognisable / but the houses near Fee St / a pocket has
stayed the same / the same old little houses.

On Fee St all the families' kids played together / their
names / Aunty will know.

The bush was all open / could walk to the bush through
to Geebung and Aspley / to see friends / go to school /
Geebung primary / all you had to worry about were snakes /
never wore shoes.

Geebung / camp / amongst the trees / and geebung groves /
the roads are old roads.

Nanny's warm arm / against mine / Mum and Nanny
touching / by the bickie shop / next to the butcher's / strong
deadly women / ready to / take on Chermy at peak hour /
on a Saturday morning.

Pride of knowing where every shop is / always notice a new
one coming up / know the specials / keep the vouchers /
push Nanny on the motor scooter / push Nanny along / save
for Christmas / the decorations are different each year / push
Nanny up the hill / tell your cousin you're coming over /
spend four hours looking for an outfit / go to Best&Less get
some undies / Nanny always bought you Bonds / said those
girls need the best / keep the docket / see if it fits.

Each year our bodies change / we get older in changing rooms /
we try to fit into jeans and schools that know our black /
mothers / just trying to fit in / Chermy is always home.

New swimmers / birthdays at the pool / the cinemas make
us cry sometimes.

My mum will kill me true / if I don't separate my recycling /
before I leave the food court / my brother is up / playing
pinball / he refuses to give me his tokens / and lollies / he
will be saving them / for weeks.

Westfield sacred to us / women are the gatherers / make
our houses safe / make our families safe / my mum,
grandmother, Aunties took care of me good / I never had

to worry about anything much / protected us when we were
little / we were jahjams / now we can with greater ease /
make our own mistakes.

Aunty buys me Belgian chocolates and Christmas cake every
year / we buy stuff / we need stuff / we were starving when
we walked up Meemar St / the hot grass / over the fence /
Aunty made us sandwich / and cuppa / black / always black.

Carried over shelves / and into tills / by the tide / I have
had buyer's regret / and I have also experienced lust / for
t-shirts / I will always remember / that never went on sale.

We get excited the flasher it gets / we are proud of our
Chermy / there has been so much change / and we are weary.

Haven't ever been inside Fee St / have just been carried into
the stories / stood outside / since I was born.

Ask your Aunty / she's the youngest / is your memory
going? / that's what your father says.

Best house on the street / sitting on the back steps / eating
ice-cream / Hah! / and sitting on the windowsill eating an
ice-block in the school holidays / long time ago!

The tree covers the house / now

I don't know where to go / now

Aunty says / couldn't get me off the dunny / always reading
Animorphs / one day I'll see small circles in the sky / the

aliens will arrive / in what's left of the forest / a small bit of park / compared to what it was / kidspace / a cricket ground / the grass where we took Max to puppy pre-school and he got his certificate into dog adulthood / one day the aliens will arrive / I will show my new alien lover Westfield Chermside / tell her that it is sacred and it must not be harmed / that inside are shiny things / delicate pathways / like the slight slope up to Coles / with the warm popcorn scent / all the exits of Myer / I will show my new alien lover and she will understand / my love for Chermy / you haven't lived life on earth until you've been to Harris Scarfe / and seen their prices on bras! / the brand Serena Williams likes / and met my family / my fam are pretty deadly / I want you to meet them / maybe at the Chinese restaurant / or has it closed / closing? / closed / and we'll hold hands to / the bus interchange / catch the 333.

Chermy shopping centre is one of our sacred sites / gammin!

Called these days / a major suburb / a new cbd / the first Apple store / have you seen the new food court / we haven't really started buying online.

We get excited the flasher it gets / we are proud of our Chermy / there has been so much change / and we are weary.

1867 / in the Gympie gold rush / settler-invaders got stuck going north / on way to the goldfields / found trouble in the creek / Downfall Creek.

The rain / don't feel like rain / when you're running from the car park / to the entrance / summer storms / sometimes

cause puddles on the floor / Aunty tells me not to slip outside
the book store / reminds me I'm wearing thongs / two sizes
too big.

Water birds / always birds / still / follow the water / and large
mobs of lorikeets get drunk / every night outside Chermy /
like teenagers.

From the park / across from Aunty's place / you can see the
church / the Prince Charles Hospital / and the best sunsets.

I jogged here / I swam here / like Nanny and Mum and
Aunty I also lived here / my place in Chermside / during
uni / on Kingsmill St / opposite the library / they knocked
my block down / to build high-rise / Aunty walks past /
keeps an eye out for me.

Chermy is rising / going up in the world / rising.

At Downfall Creek the whitefellas are falling / falling / and
we are rising / rising / to the air space / to the sky.

Boiling and burning

for my grandmothers

I know I'm not burning
(someone would be putting
   me out)
When I think about Nanny
(it's been a long time since   Everything because of you
   I've seen her)
I go to Fee St   because of me
(never been inside, just know
   it's important)
Take a picture
(stir the verandah up)
Sit with Aunty T and listen
(to her voice on tape)
Hold Mum's hand
(on the phone)

                     I don't feel my feelings
                     (nothing is final)
                     I remember Oma as the only
                       time I heard
                     Dad cry
                     (she's in my movement)
                     I have no street to walk on
                     (to feel close to her)
                     Is the water boiling
                     (she never saw my page)
                     It's just grief leaving the
                       body, that's all
                     (we can be difficult, and we
                       can be beautiful)

Bold & Beautiful

I feel burdened by what I forget. I need others to help me
remember.

Nanny's like my mum, she's generous and special. She'd give us
grandkids her last dollar. She'd give us everything she got.

She was real good with the one-liners. Her doctors at the
Prince Charles would tell you that.

Like one time she was rushed in after having a heart attack
the doctor said,
    'It's okay, Mrs Currie, you're here now. We'll get you a
comfortable bed,'
and she said,
    'I didn't know they had any here!'

Like when she couldn't breathe properly
Mum would hum songs she knew and hold her hand
the first thing Nanny said when she could talk again was
    'Can you stop that now, please?'

When Mum reminds me, I see Nanny in the bingo halls,
the smokers' area of the Wavell RSL, speeding her scooter
through Chermy, and in her armchair watching B&B
    We're still keeping up with Ridge and Brooke
    rolling our eyes till the next ad break

I remember Mum looking after her, and her looking after Mum, and me and my brother, this stitching of care between generations pulls us all in. Maybe this way I'll feel even closer to Nanny as I get older, and I care for Mum. That's the real story. That's my family.

The Only Blak Queer in the World

I was the Only Blak Queer in the world. I had many difficulties.

I didn't know how to tell my family.

I hadn't seen Steven Oliver *can't even* on Black Comedy yet, we hadn't watched it together over dinner. TV didn't save me.

I hadn't seen Electric Fields perform in a sweaty old meat market with a group of friends who had similar feelings. I hadn't heard Zaachariaha's deadly voice singing 'Nina'.

I hadn't yet read Lisa Bellear. And cried sitting on the carpet in the library over sharply written work that spoke to me and my experience.

I started a blog. I got many comments. People were always asking me what it was like to be Blak and Queer.

I hadn't yet started thinking about gender as a colonial construct. Or examined my ideas of masculinity and femininity.

I hadn't yet realised that my relationship was interracial. I started another blog. Thoughts about interracial queer relationships featured.

I hadn't got a crush on Kayemtee yet and listened to her track that samples Cold Chisel: *will your cruel attitude last forever?*

I wondered if my parents would ever accept my future partners, if I'd ever have the chance to legalise my relationship, have children, ask for more, not for less. Some nights were really lonely and I created Cathy Freeman as a lesbian and Prince as an Aboriginal.

I got trolled, deleted my social media accounts and the only known evidence of Blak Queer existence was destroyed.

I hadn't yet seen the doco on Uncle Jack Charles and met Blak Queer Elders who knew of a previous time Australians had to vote on the rights of a group of people. These Elders knew what it was like to hear their rights discussed by people outside of their group.

I hadn't yet worn my flag singlet tucked inside my Calvins as a gammin fashion statement.

I hadn't yet been to Mardi Gras.

I saw the white gays and the white gaze I was used to and then I saw Blak Queers everywhere and every conversation was an insight into a Blak Queer past, the street becoming a site of multi-time, the past-present beat, the future love, and forty years of Blak Queer pride spread into more than sixty thousand years of we-have-always-been-here.

My dance joined a big dance. I saw a Wiradjuri/Yorta Yorta lesbian couple who had been marching since the beginning, who chanted, 'Stop Police Attacks! On Gays, Women and Blacks!' in 1978 and they told me off for knowing fuck-all.

Every chant is a line of a continuing poem and I am learning the words.

I saw the flag sparkle, I saw gays from everywhere from Moree to Perth, I saw a Blak Captain Cook, Malcolm Cole, in 1988, the year of the first Aboriginal and Torres Strait Islander float, that float should have been the first float that year, but mob didn't open the parade until 2005, when Aunty Karen Cook and Aunty Lily Shearer walked out each with a coolamon of curling leaves, smoking the parade. The small leaf fire was started on the corner of Liverpool and Elizabeth Streets and in parade time, it never stopped.

I thought properly about what it meant to be marching on stolen land. And that Roger McKay in 1982, when he carried the flag in the march, made the point that the Sydney gays' golden mile was the unceded land of the people of the Eora nation. It was our modes of community and belonging white queers craved, and this influenced how they made their 'scenes'.

I woke up on a mattress in a queer share house with a text from the other Blak Queer asking to go on a date.

I consumed Blak Queer art, and I created it.

I saw Paakantyi/Barkindji artist Raymond Zada's work at the Art Gallery of South Australia and cried. I felt the heavy loss for all of the ones killed, murdered, missing. For the erasure of Blak Queers in every capital, small city and town in Australia.

And I told myself I was lucky to have stayed alive and counted the times I thought I would die. I began to know the stories of more and more and more Blak Queers who had died. I knew them as Ancestors.

I read Natalie Harkin's, Yvette Holt's, Nayuka Gorrie's and Alison Whittaker's writing online and in bookstores. I saw love for Blak Queers everywhere. Outside the city the sky sent me hints, the walks on Country along the river kept me safe. I saw the colours of my own heart, and they were not the colours of isolation and fear.

Acts of protection

i
handing me clothes of every colour
so I could camouflage
my desire

ii
presenting sticky paste
in cardboard boxes
fussing my brows straight

iii
showing pride in handwriting
leaving notes to find
in the kitchen

iv
picking me up from school with
puppy at your knees
giving love shape

v
driving to the sea
once a week
toeing in with caution and curiosity

vi
telling us who we are
not who we aren't
defying a fixed identity

Vinegar

Sometimes, the house is unclean.
In this panic
I find myself in both past and future.
*When we clean houses we do so knowing that they are watching
and our lives depend on it.*
*When we teach our children to clean houses we do so knowing
that they are watching and our lives depend on it.*
I honour your cleaning recipes. Squatting on the shower floor.
I will not have to work as hard and I don't have your
burdens but I wonder
does the intergenerational load get lighter or heavier?

My Country

my country
is between two rivers

two ribs
two hipbones

if I mapped it for you
it would be a narrow shape

like a trunk
the shape of me is shifting

hollowing wrists
smaller breasts

the places I notice
are losing and lacking

one hipbone
more pronounced than the other

is a long absence from country
related to my eating

is interrupted sleep
rivers with no beds

is dirt under my nails
drilling

is nausea
clearing

I let my stomach hair grow
so you won't notice

I show you my blood
goomera

runs into the sea
and is returned

my hands
push into the soil

my country and I
numb until fed

Oyster Shell Necklace

for Uncle Jim Everett and Aunty Patsy Cameron,
and respect to First Nations Tasmanian people
on whose Country I visited in 2016

I didn't fill the bay
or make the rocks
I didn't.

Hear Tassie's haunted
wasn't sure how I'd feel
I feel.

Water in your welcome
the clouds, the blood
water.

All feeds all
mud oysters, mutton birds
all feeds.

Parting gift
shell in your hands
now in my hands
on your neck
now on my neck.

Safe travel
with shell strung close
heartbeat close.

Workshop

we left crumbs on Country
forgot to bring them into our heated cars

the photo I took of you is blurry
I walked home to a spider on my bed

beneath the lamplight
the strangeness between us is glowing

I found a place in this home hip-width
with a thought to replace you

I won't flood like I used to
my kidneys are ready for winter

it's cold here
but I'm working

shut the door
I'm working

Whiteness is always
approaching

Footnotes on a timeline

Burnt in blue to circumnavigate the strange land of
evanescence, the blue line they call time moving all forward,
blueing the blackfellas they dared called savage – you
can't steal from savages. There was infinite wealth to steal.
Do you understand what it means to be a beneficiary of
colonisation? Can we creep through the timeline and draw
against the ancient–modern binary?

I can point on one side of the wave to my ancestors' story,
I trace it through. They thought they cleaned it up but they
built the shallowest grave. They sold their soul for gold and
coal and oil and we line our stomachs with water, it will
be our armour, we are the people that can live inside our
dreaming, live inside the sea, live inside a turtle's heartbeat,
live inside the sun on the sand, warm this country for
centuries because we are the real entities.

Don't turn a blind eye, please, all we need for you to see is
that climate is our only bank. If we don't have healthy water,
air, earth, we got nothing. So where does your money go,
where does your time go? My time and your time are on this
timeline.

There's time for us to read out all of the footnotes, go over
the fine print. They burnt records of us in fires, they stole
the evidence of our survival. But check my blood, I'm from
here. This country is a haunted house, governments still
playing cat chasing marsupial mouse. How many lies on
your timeline? Have you ever felt like you're just killing

time? We're still smoking sores. Let's carbon date it, baby. We have time to read out all the footnotes of a timeline in Reckitt's Blue.

A ship-shaped hole in the forest

Such a sad sight: a ship-shaped hole in the forest
still recovering from the fright of colonisation
the straightest pine cut into masts
elm into keel and stern post
white oak into hull, floors and futtocks
for the farms: streams of straw and cattle
grazing on the deforested floor.

While the ship sails in southern seas
the ship-shaped hole
thousands of years deep
aches and aches
the people burn their furniture to stay warm
try to regenerate with new trees
left with commercial forests
and waldsterben.

No consent was asked from the materials of 'discovery'
in Yugambeh our names for boat and
tree that makes the boat are the same
material handled with care
spirit lives
in the same name
so do I call you tree or mast
as I walk through the wood
full of so many ship-shaped holes?

'Postcolonial' musings in Urup

like the snake who ate
a kangaroo

Urup colonised itself
      and now has a belly ache

        local languages
        hang in the balance

the river pushed
for commerce

        coffee grounds on the
        railway tracks

        cotton seeds
        in the air

        merchant houses
built on backs

wolves asked
        welcome back

beavers needed
        to clean the river

        red squirrels
        fend off the greys

migrant children play football
on the hills

gold-draped buildings
fester in the city

on our land, their traditions honoured
why aren't ours?

let's get the U-Grip
off our Dhagun

Funeral Plan

what can you do with your body?
it's just one body

when history becomes necessary
the sadness belongs to me

I am not aware of my power
you watch me build my weapon

Call a Spade a Spade

a heart a heart
a diamond a diamond
a club a club
call it invasion not settlement
call it genocide not colonisation
call it theft not establishment
don't call January 26 Australia Day
don't shy away from telling the truth
don't say 'no worries' say 'I worry'
for the future of our country, our environment
if we fail to listen and to act
don't say 'we're full'
say 'we're open'
call yourself an ally
call yourself a mate

Sacred ground beating heart

sacred ground beating heart
ancient sound feeding art
we're all sleeping on a sensation
bigger than us, bigger than the body
if you roll me I'll be thunder
if you squeeze me I'll be dance
move, jahjam, move
put your feet in the earth
recover yourself
don't stop dreaming
softly spin
all the way around
ancient sound feeding art
sacred ground beating heart

Water power
for Aunty Mel

when I feel dominated by the
black cone spike in my belly
I remember the strength
of freshwater and saltwater
the path it leaves inside me

starting with just one river
in my hand
water power
drives the spike off

I'm slowly recovering
my water
I'm slowly recovering
my power

I was a perfect GF

but sometimes I was black

Type

I don't know your   blood type
Is it A-B-O?

I don't know your   background
Is it ¼?

I don't know your   softness
Can I hold it in my hands?

Expert

poor me
don't know how it happened
think I got
a non-Indigenous girlfriend
who thinks she's an expert
don't know how she got her expertise
think I'm the first one she's met
yet
she tells me I'm closed to other sides of the debate
that she has the answers because she saw a television ad
for Recognition
and though most Indigenous Australians are opposed
she says it's for our good
talks about drunks and sexual abuse 'up north'
devalues my own knowledge (too urban)
and anything I get from black media
(not the whole truth
I wouldn't trust it)
she likes to argue when she's had a few
13 times more
her voice loud
(87%) of intimate partner homicides
fresh tears on my face
involving Indigenous people are alcohol-related
she's drunk, I tell the booliman
still shaking. Sitting on the steps
no, I haven't had any
won't let her forget this statistic
tonight it's her
in the paddy wagon

The Last Apology

Let this be the last apology
that moves from your lips
I don't want your flowers
or your cheek kisses
I don't want your words
my hands move to my ears

You want to make up and make out
you don't want to promise
you won't do it again

It must never never happen again
you said ten years ago
we are truly equal partners
with a beautiful future ahead

Let this be the last apology
that moves from your lips
I don't want your flowers
or your cheek kisses
I don't want your words
my hands move to my ears

You want to make up and make out
with the Aboriginal flag
I want you to promise
you won't do it again

Women are still not being heard
for Ms Dhu

women are still not being heard
our bodies ignored
crimes against us approved
sister spoke up
it took her life
in custody, without custodianship
children taken, and land
weeping and lonely
no more women unheard behind the wall
no more women dead over unpaid fines
no more women dead by men
it must end

Whiteness is always approaching

      guilt makes people interesting

I found out Indigenous Studies has nothing to do with me

ecopotent

tidda asks me
to pen poems
for Yugambeh translation

                                    could do but
                        if it wasn't for colonisation
                    wouldn't have anything to write about
                                        trugod

dugai asks me
to pen poems
for ecopoetics journal

                                    whatttttt
                        you think words will save trees?

some hipstas love blaks
some have never
heard of us

                                    sorry can't
                        don't want to write another
                    Indigenous bio 50 words or less
                            my headshot's corrupt

label your art ecopoetic
I think it really is
ecopornographic

                        just call me ecopessimistic
                        kick me out of the conference

Gubbaleaks

my tiddas & I
gubbaleak
over dinner

share intense exchanges
verbal abuse
in our inbox

screenshots
of the hot shots
who think they own our careers

what makes gubbas
think they can get away with
disrespectin

our bodies
cultures, elders, communities, lands?
we owe them nothing

all racism leaks & streaks
don't let us be the only ones
who see the stains

In this community
Boonwurrung Country, June 2017

mutual suspicion
in this community
whitefella-owned homes gated & locked
blackfella-rented house magpie-guarded
sugared study afternoons
walks at dusk
scaling fences & stretching thick-grassed vacant lots
trespassing to find the ocean
waves eating activewear
sand lining lycra
not in Aus, mate
bad things don't happen here
our beaches are open
they are not places where bloodied mattresses burn
through roads & gates
slip teatree shapes
on the way home a need to ask
if we feel free

Snakes

7. You feel insecure about how your writing might be read under a white gaze.
6. You are told you may be offended by some of the other stories in the collection.
5. You are the only Indigenous person they have approached for the project.
4. Payment has not yet been guaranteed.
3. Editor calls the project a word in an 'extinct indigenous language'.
2. Lower case 'Indigenous' or 'Aboriginal' is used.
1. Editor mentions she went out with 'one' once, you remind her of him.

Ladders

1. The gig is paid.
2. Supa included.
3. The deadline is a little soon but you think you can move some things around.
4. You think you might have freaked them out a little bit.
5. You are not the first 'one' they have worked with.
6. You make it through the first draft.
7. Aunty calls to gossip.

it might be wonderful if she come rally with me one time
people are always changing and growing
I can picture it, us under the black yellow red flag!
it is not your responsibility to teach her though
she go to that women's rally but not a black rally
sounds like there is like a huge political dissonance
maybe you can give her a bit of reading?

Portrait of Destiny

I don't live as an artist.

> – Destiny Deacon, 1996

Kuku   Erub/Mer   woman

       sharp   strong   relational

history   politics   photography

       performance

radio   video   installation

       finding   bringing the dolls   home

thanks   Sis   for dropping the 'c'

for us urban blaks   you gave us a way   to break

free   from their expectations   define our identity

       on our own terms

thanks Sis for taking the   *white people's invention*

    putting your blak eye   behind the lens

      representing us

you know   I also feel   when I'm sitting on the

couch   I am always feeling   too much

telling stories sometimes   is the only way out

Brunswick Sista   wherever you are

    lounge   living room   Island

darkroom   gallery   lecture hall   classroom

you're deadly

    Sis   too deadly

White Excellence

after Thelma Plum's 'Woke Blokes'
and Aunty Kerry Reed-Gilbert's 'Visitors'

When it comes to having white people in my life, I choose the cream of the crop. Not your average 'woke bloke'. I'm talking about White Excellence. White people at the top of their game. You know, the ones you meet and you're like, *who's trained you?* If you're a whitefella in my life, you have gone through a very rigorous selection process. Congrats! And tbh babe, I'm still testing you.

White Excellence comes in many forms but my favourites are the ones who cook for me. Listen, make space. Buy black books, buy black music. Never assume to know what we think or what we want. Have the difficult conversations. Pick up the slack. Share the physical and emotional labour. White Excellence acknowledges other ways of being. White Excellence should be a filter on Tinder. White Excellence makes good guests because they know they are permanent Visitors.

Pleasure Seeking

What if the ancestors are watching us fuck?
                                    – Malcolm Tariq

Babe, you're not gonna find good sex tips in the search bar
it's a colonised capitalist space
all the first hits are white
you're just giving them your data

You need a Sista to lead you astray
tell you if you push your fingers just so ...
she'll always be ...
she'll always be ...

Wait, what are *you* into?
hot consent, antiracist love, deep feelings
politically progressive desire and negotiated risk
okay!

In the t-bar position
your maps transpose
land sea sky
occupation re-occupation decolonisation

Tell her ...
go'n, tell her ...
you're not really dating
unless you're dating each other's ancestors

Four truths and a treaty

1.
We gotta talk about sexism, homophobia and transphobia
in the community. No point pretendin it don't exist.
Some fellas feel threatened by young women speakin up.
Threatened by gay men and women speakin up. Threatened
by gender-diverse mob speakin up. Lemme tell you, we have
every right to be here. You gotta call this shit out when you
can. Don't fool yourself in believin 'lowkey' homophobia
is just a part of life. You don't know what kid is gonna feel
alone in their room afterwards. Be part of the vision for
a better world. Discrimination and abuse is not part of
culture. We have a place for everyone. More diverse we are,
the stronger we are as people. I'm not gonna tiptoe around
his fear. I'm not calling him 'Uncle'.

2.
I get onto them Lifeline mob when I feel like I might do
somethin to myself. No shame eh, that's what they're there
for. Mental health is just like physical health. If you're sick,
you get help. I'm lookin after myself so I can look after my
community.

3.
Wish those pollies would start their speeches with
'everything I'm gonna say from here on is a lie'. Would
be honest eh? They are always lookin at givin us the bare
minimum. They'll talk themselves out of the deepest hole.

4.

I've looked at a fair-skinned one and wondered where they fit in. Infected by gossip and identity-policing. Please forgive my lateral violence and internalised racism. I have no right to judge.

TREATY

OF

SHARED POWER

BETWEEN

Throat's

Reader

and

Author

X ——————————————————————

2020

I don't want this to go into the pile of broken treaties. If there is a need to formalise a relationship between the parties I'd like to do so in poetry.

English is the requisite language of this treaty but ideally the agreement would be tabled in Yugambeh.

Here we recognise my Country was invaded not civilised. We recognise my sovereignty and agree that I exist independently of the Australian Government and I am capable of entering into agreements without government intervention.

I'm not sure whom I'm entering into this agreement with. Are you whitefella, blackfella or a fella of another colour? Whose Country do you belong to and whose do you occupy? What is our relationship with each other? What are our expectations of each other?

Does this treaty cover the time you spend with this book or does it go further?

What of UQP's claim? Does the fact that I have entered into an agreement with a non-Indigenous-owned press complicate this treaty? What about the non-Mununjali Yugambeh people employed in the production of this book? Does their involvement allow them a share?

Who is the custodian of this book?
How do we co-exist on this page?
How can we re-imagine custodianship?
Is this an agreement or a series of unanswered questions?
Are you willing to enter an agreement that is incomplete and subject to change?

The body labours under memory

My tongue hurts
from all the things I have said
all the things I haven't

Ways of feeling invisible
require
proper planning

All the spit in the world
in this pool
especially mine

Queens

for Candy Royalle

Read my terms and conditions
we all carry wars within us

There was a time where
I was into perfection
I was outside myself
the spiritual work
didn't get done

I learnt to fear fear
I buried mountains

I didn't know that I was just beginning
and all of our stories are really about finding a
connection that will help with the pain

And that we all lead back to rivers
and flow into sea
and we breathe with our mothers
and heartbeat with our grandmothers

Despite what is against us
we make excellent choices
and are deserving of the fullest and warmest love

This is the time of night
where we can ask ourselves
how much would
we do without fear?

*I can't wait to
meet my future
genders*

Body Flow

The POOR GODDESS has a body like me.
Maybe
I'm in the WONDERFUL CITY
walking around, I see a
hip and leg wrapped around a whale
half bodies
star-shaped arrangement of limbs
legs everywhere
hippos suspended on a raised platform
this city is ugly
I should leave.

I guess it would be fitting to describe my body here.
Spidery
flowy
nothing to hide
hips in the wrong place
unambitious arms
wish my t-shirt fit the way it does
on the young M volunteer
need to work out
these shoulders
the young F volunteer
is wearing those boots I wanted last year
her legs look so tiny
mine need muscle to play football.
Hers are muscly too but slight.

The first time I heard 'they' with my name after 'her'
I said the second felt more right
her arm across my body
I think about the time we ran
she put the netball in my hand
and showed me how to move
in three steps
ankles matter just as much
in football.

Bodies are vessels but mine does not float well
I sit with the NEW BOOK OF MOUNTAINS AND SEAS
think of my tits, itchy under
I follow the narrative as it speaks to me
shovel bodies into a pit
create an ash pile
rats skate down the tunnel
water comes
everything under
the stars don't go back
as soon as you think of leaving, leave.

HOMOFOMO

Maybe You?
(Dutch)
145 minutes
Adapted from the award-winning novel
this beautiful Dutch-language film follows the coming-out
journey of its ripening teenage protagonist. Its twenty-two
minute love scene raised much discussion from critics at
Cannes, with many praising the talent (and stamina) of the
film's emerging young talents.

With Feeling
(Australia)
101 minutes
Hotter than your turmeric latte your newest classic
Australian White lesbian romance. This film sure does pass
the Bechdel test with a total of eight discussions between
cis women about eating pussy!

I Am Not My Lips
(France)
166 mins
Our opening night stunner
a sexy summer film about two beautiful young men
in expensive board shorts with well-to-do lives and a lot
of time on their hands.

Her Sister
(Greece)
134 mins
This year's tragic trans film, which again tries to convince its
audience that trans and gender-diverse people don't deserve
acceptance//friends//long-lasting partnerships//supportive
families//healthy lives
directed by a fetishist outsider
starring high-profile cis actors.

Welcome to the Inner West
(Australia)
86 mins
Touching mosaic portraits of young queer students
and their pets sharehousing in Sydney's inner-west suburbs
of Petersham and Elwood unaware of whose land they're on.

That Part of Us
(USA)
120 mins
Our pick of the films straights
will most enjoy
a gentle heteronormative dramedy featuring a familiar and
award-winning cast about coming out in later life
and the joy of neoliberalism.
It's our closing night must-see event!

Electrifying
(UK)
134 mins
Featuring the 'most kinetic kissing scene' at this year's festival
a women's circus teacher struggles with passionate feelings
for a mysterious
young trapeze artist in
1980s Southend London.

Across the Sky
(USA)
212 mins
Described as '*Brokeback Mountain* in space' by *The Guardian*
this genre-breaking film brings denim shirts to Mars for the
first time
and also has good CGI.

Water on Water

The music of the water as it coves. We covet each other. Rings from the aquarium gift shop that change colour. Cover of sunlight does not show what happens after dark when the neighbours stone the penguins to death on the beach, leave them with coffee cups over their heads to drown. She wears my hoodie over her eyes as she lies on my lap on the rocks above the water, and says we have both been under and over and beside, today, and maybe she is suggesting we will also be in the water, when we return to the city. That pool by the harbour, the drama of water on water. It is not loud if it is dying. If we have brought a species to extinction let it flood and fill our minds with sound. There is always the anxiety of airports and trains where hands slip, where unnecessary promises are made, where the views we shared just go, just leave us until we can pick them up again. This time of year the trees keep giving us things: wattles, hibiscus flowers, banksia seed pods. I am loved.

Blood Sex Mentorship

She gets an email from an older lesbian writer praising her on the sex scenes in her novel. She knows this writer has given sex as mentorship before. She herself has received sex as mentorship before.

She fantasises about being dominated by this woman, and being tasted by the woman's (expert) tongue. Every artist she knows has gone through this initiation.

When she starts sleeping with Y, her cycle changes, in order to bleed closer to Y. This means she is premenstrual when Y is menstrual. She dreams of creating a joint menstruation chart, she believes it is the map of the world. Blood is as preciously desirable as sexual secretions. She tells Y she wants her blood inside her. They read Maggie Nelson and talk about writing each other, as Maggie writes Harry. Y requests she hold her as she pours the blood from her moon cup down the sink, and she sees this moment in fiction before it is realised. Not yet does she know what is private, where the trip lines are.

Horror (plural)

unconscious knowledge
anti-colonial doubt
instinctual complicity
loss of self-language
dark emotional labour
faceless respect
rural–urban ignorance
some systematic version of ourselves
radical mistrust
gender terror
institutional voice
acceptable bias
rigid unknown

a reminder of love
sent from my iPhone

Bonsoy

I brought my own Bonsoy
it tastes better
than the nut stuff

sometimes I get sore or dull or
scared when you touch me
even when you don't

sometimes I just want to know this body
can be enjoyed by someone
not necessarily myself

I have told you so much about
a river you haven't seen
love is easy, trust is tougher

sometimes I want to create a dictionary together
because this body is rejecting the common names
and the common ways

I am discouraged from using
too many descriptors
but they make good endings

juggling shame, guilt and alienation
with the desire to
feel free, connected and powerful

Dysphoria

liberate love
into dust
shifting, self-gearing
love them all
credit me
do what makes you happy, she says
but doesn't mean it in the way my mum says
the desire to take clothes off
to take them off but also take
off another layer underneath
peel away those expectations
get closer to my truth
I love my mind but I haven't come to terms with this
I catch you in an embrace with another part of me
looking backwards
into dust

Nothing started the day I was born.
No gender or story.

No walls went up.
I was quiet.

Engaged

I'm all about love
Today I want someone to
present me with a sticky-tape
ring
dazzle me with words &
&
&
I never thought it could be me
I'd like to be engaged
in these hours
before the decision
I'd like to be engaged
for a day

The Queer Heatwave

this heatwave will not end
until I spend the night in her grip
the city gets hotter
knows I'm hard
moody, craving electrical skies
no Australian Open or cherries can distract

people lining up on the streets to get married
yeses fading
cafes re-opening

when the heat breaks
I will stumble with my change
pay the driver
see flashes of everything
childhood, home, exes, death
things that mean something

people lining up on the streets to get married
yeses fading
cafes re-opening

clouds hide the sky
our stomachs twist
the pretending
the unpretending
the chance to finally name a need
and name it with cries

people lining up on the streets to get married
yeses fading
cafes re-opening

for now
the sheets are cold
her heartbeat's running like a fridge
I think my first
clear thoughts
of the year

Questions of Travel

when we travel
we become feral
aggressors of change
threats to the balance
of the native environment
try to limit ourselves to
minimal movements
quiet words

when we travel
we become feral
we allow ourselves extra sleep, meals
and drink
shirts wrinkle in backpacks
sunburn shadows our face
insects dimple our arms
we walk with a cultural limp

Questions of Love

in South-East Asia, my appearance
allows queers to feel comfortable
to speak to me openly
about what is not open in their country
some have been closeted for decades
fearing rejection from family, loss of employment
and violence, they adopt complicated codes of secrecy

I feel honoured to have these conversations
over fish or coffee
we speak about gender before colonisation
we speak about love before colonisation
remembering-forgetting-knowing-needing
we are bleeding from the same temple
sharing the same ocean

Questions of Home

Will you take my Aboriginal passport on arrival?
Will you take my tears as proof of identity?

I have nothing good to say about my country on this plane.

I brace myself so much on arrival
I forget to breathe.

Silenced identity

I think about those murdered and missing
counted, described and spoken about
in courts and in tabloids
without their true gender identities
dissected, violated, robbed and autopsied
no affirmation
no justice
continuing violence
every night and in every silence
I watch and listen out for you

Future perfect

My future love, sometimes everything
feels like it's opening, and then it's
shutting. Breathing into the house
so it knows me. Making protective
circles out of string.
My friends, come over and pick
olives from the tree.
Let's make this
the most exciting day.
We'll remember
my heart as a t-shirt
ripping under the arms.

speaking

outside

breeze
flows

leaves
fall

smoke
curls

love fuels
our step

tread lightly
like a bird

walk to water
speak in footprints

together
listen
break
heal
tap
write
bleed

living loving
on sacred land

Together

we come together now
clanswomen and women
from other nations to laugh
and to cry

my mother, my aunt, my niece,
my sister, you are mine, we're all
together now
through sorry time

and happy time and
silly time, goanna time
and yabby time
we are one camp

Listen

keep the children safe
tell them story, same story
keep 'em grounded

in this circle
we will be heard
we will be understood

I want everything for my people – that's our way
she will know more when I pass – that's our way
I call her all of her names

I love you
even though I'm yet to meet you
I'll see you soon

tell our strong young women
talk up, bub
like your mother and grandmother are at the table

Break

we are the divers
tumbling our bodies
through water
with open hands

the diggers
of pencil yam

the transmitters
you hear our voices
all over country
amplifying the whispers

the keepers
of skin

the weavers
of bags
and covering
protection

we are instincts
we are rain

strong back
for hard work
strong heart
for soft work

the backbone of land
women's space
for love
for beginning

Heal

we are cleaning out the same rock holes
our old people did

we heal with food
and song
and medicine

we come round you
hold you up
when you can't stand on your own

the harvest
and then the feast
of mullet
and lemongrass

the scent
will cleanse the air

we cut skin
where the bite
loosens its poison
seal with coal

we heal hearts by crying
mourning our mothers
our heroes
the sky is black with geese

Tap

sticks
bounce in my hand
one end
following my mother
other end
my child following me
we have the same hurts
make fire
to reconcile
join that song
been there
when we were small
when we were old
tap sticks by the fire
feel like coming home

Write

we are not safe
from those 'in the know'
at the pub, on the footy field
the lift home, the job interview
favours become threats

don't tell me I can't write the wrongs
don't tell me I can't
in the face of this be strong
or why we can't all just get along

old people, old country. deep prints
longtime. longtime yet for you to know
us. and for us to know our future

Bleed

we are close
we will be closer
we are close
we will be closer

Crushed

for Mum, a library woman

A trip to the library
Can transport you to another dimension
All the questions you've wanted to ask
It's in the bag
A full range.
A zen-like space.
Search, Like, Share!
The book:
Provides a useful accessory
An intimate way to travel
A peaceful drift along a river
All my crushes
Have been books

I do have a tongue
      that wants to speak
            in the language of cultural desire

I want so much more

Which part of the
      brain   body   throat
         does language enter?

Tell me what happened at the opening

What does it mean to be held
           in another
              tongue

Bahbuny,
I wanted to speak to you in our language
and tell you I love you

        Stars broke
        when they heard you died
        dust fell at our feet

Gamay yarga,
why you keep me awake
is it to teach me I am not alone

Guwany,
why you keep me awake
is the night like day to you

Gibam garandalehn,
why you keep me awake
what am I still to do

take the feather
over the bird
dream in song

make music
jagunu
sing in dreams

Gumerahla
wanyi
ngay

Mum says
it sounds like a child wrote it.
Yes, I'm still a child,
I was eleven when Nanny passed.
I do not have adult words.
I am sorry for my bent and buried tongue.

All that is loved (can be saved)

for Norman

you might find
language is inside you

shiny and speckled like a rock
that wants someone to sit on it

you might find
instead of an empty silence

your ears filled
with wind and sound

birds hold conversations
thousand years old

your loves love your ancient thoughts
they have come to you

it could be a house
it could be the wrinkles

in the hands of a man
who knows your grandfather

it could be a rain cloud above
an equally promising body of water

when you speak
you are in listening

when you dream
you are in dreaming

close your eyes and feel the space
what is it saying?

it could be what you do
when you are broken

it could be what you do
when you are safe

you might find
language is inside you

shiny and speckled
a rock

*take me to
the back of
my throat*

this deadly love
for Tid

Nothing flash ehhh just the story of a Mununjali Yugambeh
shapeshifter from Black Soil Country in South East QLD
fallin in big-one love with a deado Ballardong Noongar
tidda from York in south-west WA n somewhere along the
way or maybe still in progress learnin to fall in low-key love
with their own blak kweer
soul.

Culturally, I can't be without you. For my blood and
bones are fused with yours. Blood and bones – I know.
This dream will fit nicely with the one about my laundry
door – suddenly fixed. I never thought my landlord could be
so attentive to my domestic desire – the one where you and I
call each other
home.

homoe

n. homosexual domesticity
at home with your homo

she blowdries her hair the same time as vacuuming
she thinks the leaves are coming in
she wears orange as if it is home, if not home then a home in
    knowing
she means what she wants when she says her time has passed
she asks me to take her skirt off when we kiss in the spare
    room
she asks me to put ½ teaspoon more cream in her coffee
she asks me how I feel when I wake and she is all I feel
she lives in water like water is our author
she holds my hand with three fingertips and a thumb
she misses a spot as she vacuums and she returns

I used to have a name (for this)

I'm a long way from Mununjali land
gum leaves under my pillow
smuggled interstate by mouth
they are crinkled and
get smaller each day
I want to grow and get better
but I trip, love misery
care too much
always, since school
when my first light introduced
me to music and I fell
in their shadow
as I fall into yours

I used to have a name
I want to relax again

'our places' are nothing flash
inner-city Naarm
QV and the kebab shop on Sydney Rd
I'm drawn there as if memory
can save me
as if all I need is
one deep sniff
of you and it'll all be good
tonight my friend called my heart
a marathon runner
and me a chain-smoker who refuses
to quit even when their organs shut

think she meant it
as a compliment?

paths are printed in my blood
when my hope breaks
I'll have the river

unsent txt msgs

U arouse me more than the internet

       kinda just wanna listen to Feist's Pleasure & make
       out w u

I will love u till the indigo in yr jeans bleeds & fades

       I will be sitting next to u until u stand

won't be the only time u have me with my jeans off, can
guarantee

       walked into a tree thinking bout u

push against my leg pls

       i want yr rhythm & yr pace & yr space & yr heart pls

bbe?

The cities that ate Australia

Sydney piled sand on the canvas and called it safe harbour.
Melbourne curated the trees and called it culture.
Brisbane cleared the sky of butterflies and called it sunshine.

We get lost in these galleries.
Leaving pieces of ourselves in the cloak room.
Probing for the exit sign.

They make us feel like we should be so grateful just to be
here.

Terra Nova

long butterfly
pacy sky

this place turned
into what themfellas imagined

the rainforest is ulterior motive
the air is no good

we know how to be sick
we've seen a lot of movies

tears dyed fabric
we made for our houses

themfellas named this Terra Nova
they didn't make it easy to believe

we know this well-learnt place is the home of cockatoos
even though they have gone

the only birds are mascots of the Games
found in abandoned servos, in her hands

ancestors still throw nets
over the fluorescent river

long butterfly
pacy sky

she spoke about hope
until I believed

she would come back
with answers

Offline

all the weather warnings say 'stay inside'
lying still on the floor
radio around neck
there is power in information
though data can be manipulated
was this memory politically planted
fed to my body?
are we stuffed full of truths
to stay lonely?

QLDR

How do you find the words to tell the story of the
environmental emergency of our times?
                              – Alexis Wright, 2019

I come bk & climate loses the election
& I describe to my hypnotherapist

deep heat from my feet upwards
at soccer trg

mob down south quick to pile on
happy to b hme

in dutton's electorate
18 yos tell me they r votin

for their future
my tongue bites bk

far north, north, central, west & south
east where my heart

beats thru shuttles
runnin to b home

state of peerless complexity
tidda environment minister & adani

who takes?
black throats & black-throated finch

shadow of blame
risin fire legs

lost my generation
to spotify

each time I speak with
our old ones they die

dnt b shame ur from
here sacred duty calls

stronger in the sun
state tellin story

who speaks?
QLDR QLDR QLDR

Politicians having long showers
on stolen land
written on Latji Latji, Paakantyi/Barkindji and Jarijari Country

the Minister for Agriculture
is having a long lazy hot shower
knees starting to
burn, she adjusts the temperature

more than forty First Nations
belong to the Murray–Darling Basin
rivers stretch like hands
across our continent

depending where you live
you are
or soon will be
gung djam – without water

the Minister of Energy and Emissions
is scrubbing his pits clean
about to change into a new suit
for the third time today

the Minister for Water Resources, Drought, Rural Finance,
Natural Disaster and Emergency Management
is pondering life's big questions under the showerhead
steam rising

if a couple of frogs got to die who cares
we'll make sure we
have the comfort we deserve
squeeze out every last drop

tell ya what, we're experiencing a drought alright, a drought
of thought
water sold offshore, cotton and rice don't belong here
forests and birds gone for good

one million fish screaming the same thing
listen!
these river systems been looked after
for thousands of generations

mob're gung djam to drink
mob're gung djam for dialysis
mob're gung djam to wash their bubbas
mob're gung djam to live

the Prime Minister
is whistling a
familiar tune
over the heavy flow

blue-green algae blooming
attaching to his big toe
steady streams waning
fading down the drain

When I was sick, I imagined knives coming out of backs and into each other's stomachs, I imagined days where the sun was swallowed by the first train, never to return. You were my breakfast and death and I couldn't do anything with or without you.

take me to the back of yr throat
                      I'll stay
take me to the back of my throat
                      I'll stay

Carnal injury

This is where it hurts

where I love

got a barcode

only be scanned by you

my diagnosis

your fear

we both can't sleep

I grieve in sleep

I sleep topless
imagining my lover by my side
I kiss their cheek and hold their tired body
and here my dysphoria fades and my eyes shut
as I ask them to unwrap secrets of their day.

It's been weeks and months and soon will be years.
They haven't called or written or kissed me in so long.

My friend
insists this lover has gone. This love is gone.
My spine keeps me here. *It's not over.*
How can it be? Not while the butterflies are still breathing.
Not while I still have crushed eucalypt in my hand.

Paper ships

I know what you're thinking
    how can we save the world?
      when we have barely
        just survived it

when we have been disposed of
   raped and murdered
      erased and orphaned
        and lost 90% or more of our kin

when we are just getting to our feet
   when we are hurt
     and barely breathing
      from the impact

when we have been dispossessed more than once
   more than twice, by killings, disease, poison
     mining companies, governments, floods
     and White fire

Aunty and Uncle fight to stay
   on their sacred land
     they won't leave
      but we don't see them on TV

can you guess two 'c' words
       so closely connected, they are the same?
              Cook and *c...*? nice try.
                    colonisation and *climate change*

fight one and you fight them both
       we *endeavour* to save this world
              guided by elders restoring
                    old science and medicine

a flame burns at the Tent Embassy in Kamberra
       still burns
              this fire represents many fires
                    reminding us we are still here

Australia marks the 250th anniversary
       of a landing in two views
              the view from the ships
                    and the view from the shore

when we imagine the shore
       we imagine our men
              holding spears, watching
                    the tall ships come closer

and our womxn?
        I've been looking for you
                I find you in the absence
                        I go back home

feel the strong defence of Country
        through the blood
                and placenta
                        of my grandmothers

with tears in my eyes
        with determined bones
                the blood seeps through
                        and speaks truth

the ships my grandmothers saw
        didn't stay in the sea
                250 years of shipwrecks
                        and inhaled smoke

it takes all of our hands
        to cast the settler imaginary off
                lift the masts off
                        out of the dirt

this is everything I've learnt about paper
                    it comes from trees
                                the tree and us are one
                                    we breathe together

we look after trees
            like they look after us
                        some are our ancestors
                                we belong to them

we give to trees
            to receive
                        they are our life
                                    and death

we never forget
            they are in the paper
                        we wear
                                crap on and write

our shelter and healing
            words mean nothing without action
                        language is empty
                                    without ceremony

Pose

Our descendants are watching. Watching us IRL,
not through a screen. There is no need to smile if we don't
want to but pose, pose, pose, because pose indicates purpose.
Let our future be our past and our past be our future.
Our descendants are our dependents. These descendants use
that digging stick to pull out them weeds, they take that
basket to carry tucker to give to their family. They take
that coolamon to carry water from that river, that's well-cared
for now. They hold it above their head to shelter from the
rain. We are living for them, we have crafted this for them.

Sand

We sat up singing. Covering our feet from the cold.
The sand I carry in my heart is hot. The
shadows are wet.

My heritage is to honour those in my
blood. We will not tire now. The song
will keep going in us.

Notes

The book's epigraph is from Patience Agbabi's 'Serious Pepper' in *R.A.W.* (Gecko Press, 1995). Reprinted with kind permission.

'Memories sometimes come backwards' is after Qwo-Li Driskill.

'18Cs' refers to Section 18C of the *Racial Discrimination Act 1975*. The poem also references Claudia Rankine's *Citizen*.

'logonliveon' is a companion piece to Quandamooka sister Megan Cope's *The Empire Strikes Black* in the exhibition Great Movements of Feeling, curated by Zara Sigglekow and shown at the Gertrude Contemporary. Ellen van Neerven and UQP acknowledge Harold Thomas as the creator of the Aboriginal flag.

'The Only Black Queer in the World' celebrates forty years of Sydney Mardi Gras and 60,000+ years of sexuality and gender diversity. This poem references Gurung and Ngugi woman Kayemetee, now performing under the name Kaylah Truth.

'Footnotes on a timeline' is after Dale Harding's painting *Wall Composition in Reckitt's Blue*.

'Sacred ground beating heart' is after Judy Watson's painting of the same name.

'The Last Apology' refers to the ten-year anniversary of the

National Apology to the Stolen Generations delivered in 2008 by then Australian prime minister Kevin Rudd.

'Women are still not being heard' refers to Ms Dhu, a 22-year-old Yamatji woman who died in police custody in South Hedland, Western Australia, in 2014.

'In this community' refers to the death of Ms Daley, a 33-year-old Aboriginal Australian woman who was found on Ten Mile Beach in Northern New South Wales in 2011.

'Portrait of Destiny' uses quotes from Destiny Deacon's 1996 artist talk during the 2nd Australia Pacific Triennial of Contemporary Art at the Queensland Art Gallery. Reprinted with kind permission.

'The body labours under memory' borrows its title from a line in Rozena Maart's paper 'Philosophy born of massacres. Marikana, the theatre of cruelty: The killing of the "kaffir"'.

'Pleasure Seeking' is after adrienne maree brown. The epigraph is from Malcolm Tariq, excerpt from 'Heed the Hollow' from *Heed the Hollow*. Copyright © 2019 by Malcolm Tariq. Reprinted with the permission of The Permissions Company, LLC on behalf of Graywolf Press, Minneapolis, Minnesota, www.graywolfpress.org.

'Body Flow' is after the Vile Bodies exhibition at White Rabbit Gallery.

'Horror (plural)' is after Katrina Irawati Graham's Feminist Horror workshop.

'Engaged' was written the day before the results of the 2017 Australian Marriage Law Postal Survey were released. 61.6% of Australians voted 'Yes' to the question 'Should the law be changed to allow same-sex couples to marry?'

'Questions of Travel' is after Michelle de Kretser.

'Silenced identity' was written on Treaty 7 Territory in Banff, Alberta, and is dedicated to murdered and missing trans, two-spirit and gender non-conforming First Nations people in Australia and Canada.

'Crushed' is a found poem using material from an inflight magazine. And a Mother's Day poem.

'All that is loved (can be saved)' is after Alice Walker.

'Terra Nova' references the American science fiction TV show of the same name filmed on Yugambeh country.

'QLDR' references the 'Queenslander!' cry, first used by whitefella Billy Moore to motivate an underdog Maroons team at the start of a 1995 State of Origin match. The epigraph is from Alexis Wright's article 'We all smell the smoke, we all feel the heat. This environmental catastrophe is global', first published in *The Guardian*, 18 May 2019. Reprinted with kind permission.

Thank you

In 2019, two of our Aunts, both immense cultural leaders, travelled back to the Dreaming. My love and gratitude to the memory of Aunty Linda McBride-Yuke and Aunty Kerry Reed-Gilbert (Mandaang, Kuracca) who taught me so much and encouraged me in this writing journey. I feel you with us every step.

Reader, for picking up this book.

My family and friends, for your transformative love. Special mention to international friends in poetry who have broadened my insight and writing: Norman, nhã thuyên, Alvin, Martin and Cori. Julie Koi, for significantly changing my laugh:cry ratio.

Grace, Krissy and Shastra, who read drafts and encouraged. Yvette, Nakkiah and Omar, for your beautiful words of endorsement. Paula, who layered my heart with writing by WOC, including Patience Agbabi whose quote sparked the title of this work. Hannah and Timmah, for your courage and willingness to share this journey together. My First Nations communities, LGBTQIA+ communities, and poetry communities for the daily reminder – we don't need to compromise!

The Booranga Writers Centre's residency in 2018 and the INPUTS University of Bremen residency in 2019. The Neilma Sidney Literary Travel Fund, for supporting my travel to Japan in 2018.

University of Queensland Press, particularly my publisher, the determined Aviva. Felicity: editor, nurturer. Cathy, for your editing and special touches to *Throat* in-house. Josh, for another sick cover.

To the editors of the following literary journals and anthologies where poems previously appeared, sometimes in different forms or under different titles: *Reading the Landscape*; *Mardi Gras 40th Anniversary* magazine; Red Room Company's *Poetry Objects* series; *Cordite Poetry Review*; QAGOMA's website; *Poetry in Multicultural Oceania – Book 3*; *Fennel Rising*; *Wild Tongues Volume 2*; *fourW Anthology*; *Peril Magazine*; *Offshoot: Contemporary Life Writing Methodologies and Practice*; Queensland Writers Centre's *#8WordStory*; *The Near and the Far: Volume Two*; *Stilts*; Red Room Company's *Poetry In First Languages Project* (with Yugambeh interpretations provided by Shaun Davis); *Return Flight: MEL>CHC*; *Australian Poetry Journal*; *Overland*; *The Saturday Paper*; and *Living with the Anthropocene*.

Index of poems

THROAT by Ellen van Neerven
Recipient of the UQP Quentin Bryce Award 2020

About the UQP Quentin Bryce Award

The Honourable Dame Quentin Bryce AD CVO is an alumna of The University of Queensland, where she completed a Bachelor of Arts and a Bachelor of Laws before becoming one of the first women admitted to the Queensland Bar. In 1968 Quentin Bryce became the first woman appointed as a faculty member of The University of Queensland's Law School. From 2003 to 2008 she served as the twenty-fourth Governor of Queensland, and from 2008 to 2014 she was the twenty-fifth Governor General of Australia, the first woman to hold the office.

In addition to her professional roles, Quentin Bryce has always been a strong supporter of the arts and Australia's cultural life and is an ambassador for many related organisations, including the Stella Prize and the Indigenous Literacy Foundation. Across many decades she has championed The University of Queensland Press (UQP), its books and authors.

To honour and celebrate her impressive career and legacy, The University of Queensland and UQP have jointly established the UQP Quentin Bryce Award. The award recognises one book on UQP's list each year that celebrates women's lives and/or promotes gender equality. In its inaugural year, *Throat* by Ellen van Neerven received the 2020 UQP Quentin Bryce Award.